Shamma
The Dancing Flame

Dear Umar Bhai & Seemi

Love - Inspire - Capture

Regards,
Esma Ashraf
17/2/19

Candle Poems by
Esma Ashraf

∩ ARCHWAY PUBLISHING

Cover illustration by Irina Sztukowski
www.artirina.com

Author photo: Patti Hale
Chosen Moments Photography
www.chosenmomentsphoto.com

www.istockphoto.com

Archway Publishing books may be ordered through booksellers or by contacting:

Archway Publishing
1663 Liberty Drive
Bloomington, IN 47403
www.archwaypublishing.com
1 (888) 242-5904

ISBN: 978-1-4808-7405-3 (sc)
ISBN: 978-1-4808-7467-1 (hc)
ISBN: 978-1-4808-7404-6 (e)

Library of Congress Control Number: 2019903349

Print information available on the last page.

Archway Publishing rev. date: 04/02/2019

Stars be the glitter of her eyes
She showers on me.
Sunshine be the warmth of her heart
I sleep in.

My first book of love is dedicated to my mother—
Because I shine through you.

Acknowledgments

In this chaotic world of madness, our dreams sometimes start to fade. Either we lose them or they leave us behind. But, on my side of the universe, someone special didn't let these dreams waste away for me. He held my hand and took me to the land where I could wear the crown of fantasy created out of my reality. He always believed in me. He cared for my dreams and encouraged me to fulfill them. *Shamma!* The Dancing Flame reflects his dedication towards this aim. I thank him for always supporting me. He is my dear husband, my life.

I would also like to thank my lovely parents for continuously encouraging me to write. Their faith in me made me who I am today.

My last note of appreciation goes to my amazing friends for accompanying me throughout my journey of writing. My venture wouldn't be possible without their love and support.

Thank you.

Love Letter

Dear You,

I hope my passion for you prints memories to be remembered by you, but not by many.
I wish that your lust for my heart will never fade away.
It is my tale created out of your stories.
You are as real as this moonlight glancing from above to find its reflection.
When the night whirls around your palace, I know it is the spark I long for.
I crave to brighten your dull moments.
I burn to illuminate.
I yearn to be enwrapped.
I am who I am, but
It is you who inspires me to live another day.
It is you who makes me restless.
You give my soul a name, an identity.
You melt the pages of my silhouettes.

As I dance, each curve of my flame venerates in your passion.
It is my dedication; it is my affection.
I find myself in you.
I thank you for being part of my existence.

In love,

Shamma

Contents

In Love
I Dance

Shamma! Desire of a Flame

Many burn by her dazzling display.
Doesn't matter; she chooses
to live this way.
Besides this notion, a mind
ponders anyway.
Dying under the moments
of shimmery days.
Love is enkindled
to let it stay.
Moth whirling around her
to convey.

My Mirror

While glancing in those eyes,
he said,
"I see a universe full of beautiful colors
as they take me to the place where
everything is frozen, but
we are moving."

My All

Being around you
means a restless million
words ready to perform
inside my book of love.

It gives my pages a
new face, an identity,
each time I am
around you.

You are the sonnet
and my song that
live through my ink,
and I prevail
through them.

Without Wings

If you learn to rise in love,
You won't enjoy any other way.

If you learn to think in depth,
You won't know any other way.

If you learn to cry in euphoria,
You won't express any other way.

If you learn to breathe in vain,
You won't praise any other way.

If you learn to dance in harmony,
You won't practice any other way.

Infectious

When you touched
my lips, I knew it
was your desire
to try melting tears.

I let you be part
of my adventure
we were tempted for.

I was that candle
flickering in ecstasy
all day long.

By the Rose Side

Flipping through the pages
she read him, the ocean
attending to each word;
he smiled at this notion,
diving to submerge
in the poem of devotion.
Gazing to inflame spark,
he kissed the emotion,
sitting across from her, still as
the world swirled in motion.

His Name

I stare at his name to forget mine.
This is how I remember myself.

I read him softly to feel my soul.
This is how I embrace myself.

I kiss the letters to conquer mine.
This is how I liberate myself.

I erase all marks to start anew.
This is how I invent myself.

Waves

Sometimes they tease more,
sometimes less, when they
touch my skin as to explore.
Whether I crave the touch
or yearn for more,
their kisses and tender
caresses tickle my toes.
Taste the salt to absorb
the inner core.
The lusty green and
sensuous blue suck the
pulp out of my soul.
Sinking under the skin
of sand as they play
to divert me away
from the shore.
Drown me; enwrap me
inside those swirls.
Show me other contours
of the world
where turquoise lands
and lavender sets to pour.

Wish List

I wish to be free
where no constraints live.

I want to surrender
to the land of authenticity.

I hope to outlive
the immortality.

I yearn to drown
in the sea of love.

I claim to ostracize
heartless fools.

I write to introduce
you to yourself.

I dare to fear
my intentions only.

I pray to embrace
the unforgotten soul.

Euphoria

I am high on life
because I see the rain dancing
and blink only to see the colors.
When the sun bathes me in its rays,
I feel clean.
Sometimes, moonlight stares
when I am dreaming.
It is a castle of my fantasyland
where I rule to conquer.
Sometimes I wear my insanity,
sometimes peace—
I have the eyes to love
and a heart to cherish.
It is my choice; this is my madness.

Completely a Woman!

She loves with passion;
She dances in beauty.
She lives by the praise;
She melts the hearts.
She is completely a woman!

Her elegance is alluring;
Her dignity is attained.
Her love is a victory;
Her grace is impeccable.
She is completely a woman!

She fights with perseverance;
She weeps in silence.
She faces with boldness;
She illuminates the life.
She is completely a woman!

Treasure Chest

This was dredged in the heart of the sea,
The depth of kindness.

This was found on the lips of flowers,
The aroma of tenderness.

This was discovered on the arm of a tree,
The moment of happiness.

This was searched for under the waterfall,
The cascade of graciousness.

This was invented into the eyes of moonlight,
The spark of brightness.

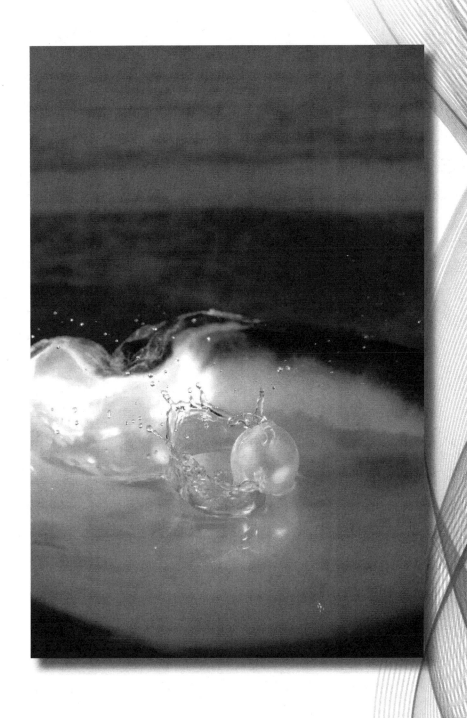

A Butterfly

Flying by the winds of color,
she feels an essence from afar
where flowers become her
home and fields become the sky.
Yellow, blue, green, and orange,
carrying shades of love in
her bosom, the clouds
kiss her palms.
Glancing through those
petals, she dives into
the streams of passion
where pain becomes her
lust and tears become the ocean.
The wind beneath her
wings, sometimes soft,
sometimes harsh, as she
glides up and above to
touch the heights.
I fly with grace; I cry in vain; I love with passion.
I am a miracle of life.

Magnetic

He was tempted to dive
into her crimson dusk,

    and

she was sinking to be
engulfed in his luminance.

Venom

He travels in me
like a drop of wine
gushes to make
one senseless.

My Calling

Happiness is:

      To love unconditionally.
      To be alive when death visits.
      To share the passion of dripping tears.
      To dive in romance.
      To see the sparkles in his eyes.

Passion is:

      To earn fragrance in his essence.
      To kiss those eyes in my dream.
      To yearn for his magic touch.
      To feel whole in his company.
      To long for intimacy.

Desire is:

      To smile only when he sees it.
      To be the taste of his wine.
      To wake up near his bedside.
      To die in his arms only.
      To whirl around his aroma.

Love Him Mad

I am too busy
thinking about
him, as there is
no time left to
waste on this
silly world.

A Shining Star

Shining through, a star
made its way to brighten
the path as she walked up
and up to spread her rays
to glorify.
She became the sky.

Today, the moon dances
in her beauty, and stars
applaud as she celebrates
her success.

Do you see it? That sparkle?
That magical show of glitters?
Don't blink, as I find it
in the heart of that precious eye, that twinkle.
I call her a shining star.

The Passage

Beneath the world of my feet,
prismatic crystals I feel.
They shine as bright as I am,
passing through the ocean,
sometimes pink, seldom ivory.
Water flows
under the surface of the iceberg.

Searching the destiny through
these frozen passages while
floating down the dancing sea,
my tears are the guiding light
as I swim through,
under the surface of the iceberg.

Glowing diamonds deliquesce
into froths on the waves as
my journey starts to search
for the paths of land where
I shall snuggle with peace surely.
But oh, the promising soul!
You must endure the pain now
under the surface of the iceberg.

Spellbound

It's your charisma
I am swayed by.
Your magical touch
makes me oblivious.
As I am under your
spell, and you have
the only power to
turn me into gold.

My Angel

Enchanting eyes, scintillating smile
Met an angel while passing by.

Gentle voice, mesmerizing persona
Met an angel while passing by.

Deep soul, alluring presence
Met an angel while passing by.

Magical touch, arresting musk
Met an angel while passing by.

Being You

Go figure! Why is it difficult to be unique?
Accept the way exceptions dwell.

Go figure! Why is it a punishment to stand alone?
Accept the way solitude fights.

Go figure! Why is it strenuous to accomplish?
Accept the way fortune manifests.

Go figure! Why is it excruciating to be heard?
Accept the way the message expresses.

Go figure! Why is it inconceivable to be eccentric?
Accept the way character shapes.

A Mermaid

Swimming under the golden sea,
She dipped deep to touch a reality,
Searched for shells, heart's sensuality,
Despite a feeling of not being free.
It was a prison, not her sanctuary.
Dreams be the ocean; waves, fantasy.
Treasure was buried without a key.
She drowned in the arms of actuality.

My Adornment

You are the veil I wear on me.
Your eyes bring spark to me.
Before sunlight kisses my shadow,
you wear that shine on me.

In the night of dreams,
I toss and turn when
your fingers dive in me.

Even my eyes won't flinch
during my sleep.
All night long,
your essence cuddles with me.

You become my skin.
The silken feel and slippery
touch immerse in me.

I don't want to wear
night, so I wear you,
and you wear me.

A Puzzle

What love is!
It can't be defined.

Where dawn sinks!
It can't be justified.

When life changes!
It can't be resigned.

What heart expresses!
It can't be denied.

How injustice prevails!
It can't be designed.

Why hate persists!
It can't be simplified.

Dream Avenue

Once sunshine said to me,
"Enter inside the candor; glare is yearning for you."

Once rainfall said to me,
"Submerge in my obsession; thunder is rumbling for you."

Once sky said to me,
"Seek beyond the limits; universe is dancing for you."

Once courage said to me,
"Rise above the fears; gallantry is searching for you."

Once heart said to me,
"Justify with the desire; love is waiting for you."

Once body said to me,
"Enfold inside my soul; tranquility is asking for you."

When It Came True

At least I lived in a
dream of his reality
and spent days of
my passion in his arms.

At least I flew by the
wind of my desires
and listened to the
beat of his heart.

At least I slept under
the moonlight and
woke up by that
shiny sky.

Temptation

I am afraid to look
deep into his eyes.

My fears may unravel
those tied knots of
lost obsessions.

Sauvignon Blanc

This wine reminds me
of a savory taste that
kissed you once.
Now, it replenishes
my pores.

Pink

Don't you see
In the style she flies?
Don't you witness
In the fashion she loves?
Don't you admire
In the extent she expresses?
Don't you approve
In the way she rebels?

Westside Highway

If we hadn't hung out
that night, I wouldn't
have come this far.

From this side to
the next, I wouldn't
have reached to where
you are.

The tunnel, a ship,
and the park
once passed by to be
ended in a bar.

We were pumped up,
standing near the door,
as our lips touched
a cigar.

Then we drove in
mania so we could
race the car.

Your eyes to mine
were as the spark
to the stars.

The route became
our destiny and healed
the broken parts.

It left these marks
on my memory, just
like bruising scars.

Silhouettes

It is my wish to
spread my rays
around you so
I can yearn more
for the petals of
your flames.

It is a sea of passion,
flowing in the heat
of your desire.
Somehow my obsession
fails to melt the contours
of your palms.

I am ignited at
the verge where
my body breaks into
dewdrops that later
turn into golden
ashes.

Love, Red, and I

My affections, your love:
contiguous they are to
behold what is yet to come,
and desires keep burning high,
so let's get drunk here.

My hands are full when I
wear the bracelet of your name.
The passion arouses in me,
so let's get drunk here.

Oh, the gushing waves
of flames want nothing
but you, and my lips
taste the sweet rosy glass
of tears.
Fresh they are for me,
so let's get drunk here.

I am empty up to the
time of fulfilment as you
pour the nectar of that
life in a dry soul to keep it going.
Alas! I long for more,
so let's get drunk here.

A Fantasy

When the eyes kiss rose petals,

The dewdrops create a fantasy.

When a ray sprinkles upon the light,

The fluorescence induces a fantasy.

When the waves caress the shore,

The restlessness awakens a fantasy.

When the scent absorbs into musk,

The romance merges into a fantasy.

When a sonnet intoxicates the heart,

The poetry embraces a fantasy.

When a dream opens a new passage,

The reality converts into a fantasy.

In Love, I Dance

I start dancing in your arms
As you play me like a violin.

I start dancing under your fragrance
As you play me like a harp.

I start dancing in your eyes
As you play me like a flute.

I start dancing on your palms
As you play me like a piano.

I start dancing in your presence
As you play me like a cello.

I start dancing on your lips
As you play me like a saxophone.

Devotion

She asks the drunkard moth,
"Why are you so foolish as to ignore your ending?"
He answers,
"No true soul without yearning loves.
No pure heart without burning melts.
This is my path; this is my destiny.
I submit myself to the arms of your flames."

In Love
I Melt

Melting Away

As the days pass
by the bedside of
blossoming flowers,
those moments
are wasting away.

I see raindrops
shattered into tiny
mirrors, trying to
find their face;
they are
dispersing away.

My skin reveals
a story of those
marks carved by
your kisses;
they are
melting away.

Irony

He once gave me a
book of gold to be kept
in my treasure chest, but
I ran out of words of jewels
for him.

The Connection

Says rose to a thorn,
"Even though my blood is gushed
from those wounds that remind me
of a pleasure, I feel to be
in your company. My passion
grows stronger, and the bond
becomes inseparable."

Says beauty to the eyes,
"Although you have ignored
my elegance at times,
I ask not to keep
that glimpse away, as you are
my mirror. And by
staring at the spark,
I feel complete."

A Void

Into the field of dreams,
Under the dusk of land,
Above the head of horizon,
By the wings of wind,
Over the thundering cloud,
I could not find you.

Building Blocks

Painful it is,
A separation!
Cruel it is,
A rejection!
Pointless it is,
An expectation!
Promise it is,
A realization!
Vulnerable it is,
An affection!
Hateful it is,
A desperation!

Wake-Up Call

It was a false act
of true love where
pain was eternal
but scars were
washed away.

Echoes

It was unnecessary,
not wanting to be
cherished, not
significant enough
to be called out, but
she stood there waiting.

Letting go was
convenient for him.
To be wasted away
was a choice, but
all she could hear was
whimpering and whining.

It Was a Fool's Paradise!

When he was done
with his story, he
left with a promise never
to return.

Dilemma

How could you resist
standing near the shore but
not diving into the ocean?

How could you resist
taking a sip from
the wineglass when it was
set on your table?

How could you resist
the wind that travels
beneath your wings and
may sweep you away?

How could you resist
to meet the eye of an
enchantress and not blink?

How could you resist
staying in a magical
land without being possessed?

How could you resist
a star shining to
light up the doorsteps
of your sky while you hide inside?

Epiphany

If I were beautiful,
He would be the admirer.

If I were a fairy,
He would be my savior.

If I were moonlight,
He would be my mirror.

If I were an enchantress,
He would be the sinner.

My Escape

I am running fast.
To where?
I don't know.

To escape maybe?
From myself or
from them. But
I am running fast.

So I can hide
in the dungeons
of my own caves
or perhaps disappear
under the mounds of
those floating clouds.

Near Sinking Waters

I fade just like an
ocean loses its color
under the reflection
of golden skies.

I sail through the
dusk to be absorbed
into lustrous shores.

I rise after each
wave pushes me
with a whisk of
sinking colors.

Autumn Fever

Some days like these
remind me of you, when
the crisp perfume of falling leaves
brings out the memories.
It was this time when
our hearts met and
our souls were connected.
You stood there,
having sparkles in
those eyes. You waited for me,
and I became whole.
Now each color of my leaf
is fading as I cross those roads,
drive by the teasing areas,
and witness nothing but
pale bodies, rotten and wounded … This is how I am
addicted to it.

Some days like these
laugh at my weaknesses
and bury my desires
under the soft pillow of
few joys, seldom sorrows.
Shattered in pieces,
just like the half-moon shining
through, doing its
best to laugh at me.
A pounding heart,
along with a rustling
sound of swishing leaves,
and then I hear nothing more.
The crisp air crushes my courage
as I walk up to search for
your footsteps; it is not you
there but dead leaves.
The time has slipped away,
but I am digging my moments
again and again … This is how I am addicted to it.

Missing Page

Look at me!
I am that torn
page of a
complete novel
that never got
to be published.

Eclipse

Too deep water is
Too deep sky.
> What is not so deep … is to die.

Too deep eyes are
Too deep heart.
> What is not so deep … is to cry.

Too deep truth is
Too deep promises.
> What is not so deep … is to lie.

Too deep feelings are
Too deep pain.
> What is not so deep … is to sigh.

Too deep sunshine is
Too deep night.
> What is not so deep … is to defy.

Ruthless Him!

Why he chose to
look the other way
when I gave him all,
My eternity.

Unripe

He left me empty,
as there was no
drink in the cup
that could quench
his thirst. Not anymore.

I was once the
nectar of his desire,
a fruit, the inebriant
of his chalice, but
not anymore.

Like an aged grape,
I am waiting for
that one moment
to be felt forever
in his mouth.
Alas! Not anymore.

Misfit

I don't belong here.
I write to vent.
I fight to get peace,
not to find myself.
I am full like a
half-moon,
counting the days of
my youth. Anyway,
I don't belong here.

I get pushed around,
so you have your way
and be the ruler, but
I don't care because
it's my casket and I
own it. Nevertheless,
I don't belong here.

I have no purpose.
I have no fate, but
I am moving along,
so each wave can
push me through
with each stride.
I taste its colors.
I don't anticipate
in the world of power,
as my heart is a slave
of freedom. Anyhow,
I don't belong here.

All Talk

It is all charm and
words that he uses to
get my attention. Otherwise,
actions speak louder than words.

Laws of Nature

Love melts
While hate is congealed.

Light radiates
While darkness takes away.

Triumph glorifies
While failure teaches you.

Day unveils
While night covers you.

Beauty personifies
While ugly stays rotten.

Falling Hearts

Crisp mornings of autumn
bring back those moments
of the sins we committed
under the canopies of
some orange, some yellow,
dying leaves.

Lame Excuses

It keeps me busy so
I go far from you, so
you don't come my way.
Sometimes I cry
and stay away from
my destiny—that is, you.

I am occupied, so I
Write to you and
dream for you.
My search becomes
my fate—that is, you.

My pain and the
notebook sleep by
my bedside.
They take me
inside the folds of distances,
where I can squelch
my lust—that is, you.

Transformation

Melt, oh heart! Just like a rock molds into the gemstone.

Blossom, oh heart! Just like a bud transforms into the flower.

Shine, oh heart, just like a darkness hides in the arms of sunlight.

Escape, oh heart! Just like a captive runs into the palms of freedom.

Cleanse, oh heart! Just like a repentance converts sins into virtues.

It's a Riddle!

Why do words fall off
from the shrubs
of autumn?

Why do gems lose
the colors of
their vanity?

Why does beauty fade
behind the shadow
of murkiness?

Why doesn't love
complete a circle
of its moon?

Why do promises hide
under the pile of
broken mirrors?

Why does the heart ignore its
perks sometimes?

Fraction

In his love,
It was some +,
maybe –
at times.
When I came
to do the
calculation,
it gave me nothing
but ?

Wilting

I am deserted
flesh glimpsing
through my window,
waiting to be
caressed by the
virgin morning.

Dismissive

What is not to be endured,
We learn to disregard.

What is not to be cherished,
We learn to lose.

What is not to be believed,
We learn to suspect.

What is not to be adored,
We learn to deprecate.

What is not to be understood,
We learn to negate.

What is not to be conveyed,
We learn to conceal.

Longing For ...

There is a world of
longing and wait.
I am there standing
still, counting so I can
see you immersing in
the moonlight rays.

I know you are there
looking for me, but
you don't say anything.
Maybe you are afraid.

But I am not as I am,
standing where you left
me under the shade of
velvety drapes.

Deep Cut

I am breaking into pieces.
Each one has a story
to tell.
A tale of victory.
A saga of deceit.

I am breaking into pieces.
Each corner is sharp
enough to paint blood
on my canvas.

I am breaking into pieces.
Each wall of my heart pines
for sunshine but rather
kisses the darkness.

Demons

Frozen in time, being unable to escape,
stuck behind the walls,
hiding under the cave.
Far away from solace,
streaming inside the wrecked sea,
I bear it all alone, fighting within.

Yes, it is a war between two
as reality or fantasy both play.
From desire to miserable soul.
In ecstasy, they make love.
Of hate, the passion lives.
I endure it all alone, fighting within.

With conviction, it is deceived.
In revenge, love is possessed.
When we bleed, we break down
where hearts have no home
and feelings are misplaced.
I inhale it all alone, fighting within.

Living a big lie, dying with guilt,
Oh, you demon! Face me now.
The truth is certain in my land.
It is not over yet, not yet, alas!
I cherish it all alone, fighting within.

Phases

Yesterday a regret embraced her with poise.
Today she asked misery to kneel down.

Yesterday her heart was in despair.
Today the hope became her limelight.

Yesterday her body was adorned with jewels.
Today she became free from the chains.

Yesterday a connection built the weakness.
Today she decided to renovate her strength.

Yesterday the romance became her vanity.
Today a dedication wore its crown.

Yesterday a fear was wrapped under the satin.
Today she chose to live with fortitude.

Yesterday her style displayed its charm.
Today the dignity polished her charisma.

Yesterday the audience laughed at her performance.
Today her fairy tale transmuted into a masterpiece.

Parallel Universe

I am stuck between
the world of dreams
and reality.

One has the power
to turn into a fairy tale.
The other becomes
real once fantasy wears off.

This is my parallel universe.

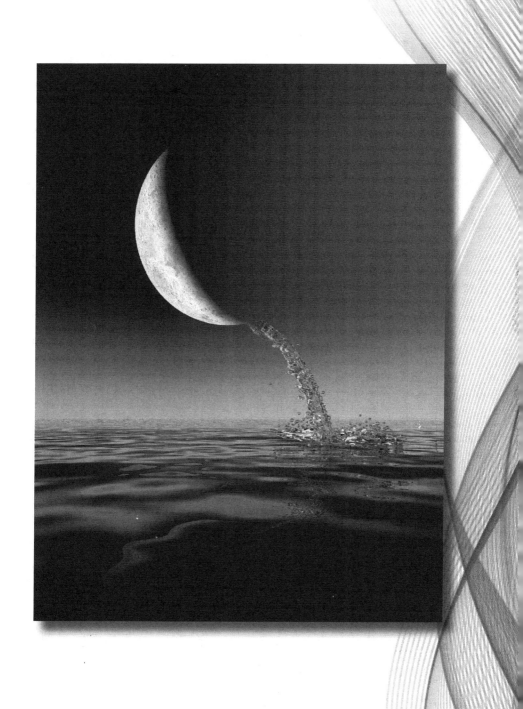

Desolate

Where is he?
She looks for his
footsteps, searching
for that heart.

As the time passes by,
the stain of his skin
is dappled over her.

She is deceived as
he has gone forever.

Carrying a memento of
him, she feels numb
sitting under a sultry
sun, waiting to be
drenched again.

A Poet's Life

He lived through her words
to be remembered by many.
She blossomed in his world
but wilted after twilight. Alas!
Myths unfolded the chariness.
Now the candor nestles within her heart.

Romance, that sweetness,
only survived through her melting pen.
Now the time has come to test the blank ink,
as the pages will now drink her red
tears and drapes of her windows
will keep the moonlight from glancing through.
The flames will mock her courage.
This is her fate; this is her life.

But wait—he hasn't left yet.
Still he sleeps by her book.
It is him, a storyteller.
She makes love to his
thoughts all night long.

Setting like a tear in her eye,
the story dissolves nevertheless.
He invented himself through her,
then vanished to search for another, maybe.

This is how the poetry evolves.
This is how the life takes strolls.
Unfortunately,
this is a poet's life.

Silent Skies

Couldn't hear any sound.
What was felt, a silence.
From one sky to another,
panting to step on.
Still remained quiet as
it was his verdict, not mine.
In absence, he breathes in,
although I screech in silence.
Oh, the soothing cadence
where his heartbeat resides
in me, but I shall keep
breathing silence.

In Love, I Melt

As you inflame my tarnished spark,
I melt like a tear to dissolve into you.

As you scorch to try a new flavor,
I melt like a hue of champagne into you.

As you touch to make me feel alive,
I melt like a seeping of lust into you.

As you whisper to say, "I love you,"
I melt like a drop of rain into you.

The End

He never loved me.
And I did nothing else
in my time of worshipping.

He never cared
for the heart made
of wax, frozen,
yielding to breathe
another day.

He never regretted to
doubt, as if I have
ever asked anything
in return.

He never cherished me
but rather punished me for
mistakes I have
not committed.

He never loved me!

Shamma